THE TESTAMENT OF THE
REVEREND THOMAS DICK

W.N. HERBERT

*The Testament of the
Reverend Thomas Dick*

PUBLICATIONS
1994

Published by Arc Publications
Nanholme Mill, Shaw Wood Road
Todmorden, Lancs. U.K. OL14 6DA

Design by Tony Ward
Printed at the Arc & Throstle Press
Nanholme Mill, Todmorden, Lancs.

ISBN 0 946407 92 4

Acknowledgements
Some of these poems have appeared in *Chapman,
Isis, The New Poetry, New Poetry from Oxford,
Other Tongues, Oxford Magazine, Password: Scop,
Poetry London Newsletter, Poetry Review, Poetry
Wales* and *Verse*.
The sequence "The Testament of the Reverend
Thomas Dick" was written during a Fellowship at
Hawthornden Castle.

Cover engraving of Thomas Dick courtesy Mary
Evans Picture Library, Blackheath, London.

"Poems from the Pitt Rivers" was exhibited in the
Pitt Rivers Anthropological Museum during
Oxford's Art Week, as part of the show *Snares of
Privacy and Fiction*, organised by Chris Dorsett.

"Dream of Buster Keaton" was first published in
Poet & Critic (USA), in 1987.

The publishers acknowledge financial assistance
from Yorkshire & Humberside Arts Board and
North West Arts Board.

"Time, then, is merely the device which keeps everything from happening at once."

Suzi Gablik

Contents

Pictish Whispers II

A Dream of Buster Keaton

"My mother was America's first lady saxophonist . . ."
"Instead of ram horns and a charming tail . . ."
"I can never speak . . ."
"The breakfast table gradually stretches itself . . ."
"Every morning I have to walk among the trees . . ."
"Can we build our thought into an animal . . ."
"In the dark rushes there is at least the hope . . ."
"The arteries harden . . ."
"The silence has left me . . ."
"We play cards . . ."

The Pictish Archive

Listen to the pages of the seasons fall
across the Grampians and Angus. Listen to
spring bring its normal hail like ink
that winter will again obliterate.
This is the manuscript on which
the Picts wrote "homestead", "village", "fort"
in their dismembered speech. Listen to
the pages of the landscape whisper as they turn;
it's like a copy of the Book of Kells from which
all traces of the text are being scraped.
The summer grass becomes a vellum on which
the hairs have all grown back.
Only their stones' old pictograms
still float upon the ploughshares' waves,
like illuminations that have been scrubbed
of colour, or like scenes from
a scattered silent film. Their symbols are
as simple as a Keaton sight-gag:
they could be shots from his
unmade *immrama*, they could be out-takes from
the *spielmannsepen* of the jumblies.
Words here have lost their command of time,
they shift like phrases from
Slim Gaillard's *Voutionary*, drift
like the spoofs caught up
in a supplement to Jamieson's
Dictionary of the Scottish Language;
as the Ogam on the stone at Brandsbutt
puts it: "IRATADDOARENS".

Listen to the emptied pages hint
at the revision of myths, the alternatives
to gospels that may
occupy the silences between
our usual Gilgameshes and Ulyssiads.
They are like the space that's been chipped out

within an elaborate frame, halfway down
the back of the cross-slab at Cossans.
The nameless fish-tailed serpents whose
two bodies provide the borders to
so many stones, enclose
the crescent and V-rod and
the double disc and Z-rod: messages
delivered to the synapses as
clear as a traffic signal
without a road. The censored panel sits
beneath, then a double rank
of proud horses and their riders,
who could be Nechtan, who could be Bridei,
son of Maelchon, who could be Resad,
son of Spusscio: "Drosten
ipe Uoret ett Forcus", as
the notes at St Vigeans explain,
"The inscription is simple but untranslatable."

Listen to the lowest frame at Cossans:
a boat is bearing something big to somewhere else;
it could be a coffin, it could be
it could be a book, it could be
a symbol stone itself.
I can hear the Pictish page still turning,
as though the letters wouldn't stick
and rattle from it as it turns.
I am caught up by
the fall of meanings;
I am pressganged into
the voyages of pages.
Whatever was removed from the central frame
has now become a symbol, not of decoding,
but of the removal of all codas,
the promise that
our definitions will be renewed,
like the lizard's tail, or
St Orland's fingernail.

The fictions shall be
our only translators,
the word is our incompetent,
our only sailor.

immrama – voyages
speilmannsepen – minstrel epics

11

Poems from the Pitt Rivers

Praise of a Whalebone

"Carved bone plaque representing a killer whale; haliotis shell inlay.
Ornament on a shaman's apron. Original Pitt Rivers collection.
British Columbia, Haida Indians. 14cm. long."

How well
the feel of speed
must have pierced
your whale
even to her marrow
to make you leap
so easily into
the shaman's shaping hands.

How well
he must have watched
the killers clear
the ice
and fasten on
their shuffling seals
to fix your jaws
in such a fluid vice.

How well
the haliotis shell
conveys the sheen
of freezing water
spirling from
those fleet flanks
and lends your eye
her hungry blankness.

How well
matched they were
spirit and swimmer
that it seems fitting
his image clings
to your fin
and his fierce face rides
in the flick of your tail.

The Hunter's Song

"Bone model of native gull-trap built of snow. A piece of blubber is tied outside and the ESKIMO, seated inside, puts his hand up through the hole in the roof and seizes the gull by the legs. The hole is covered with a mask of soft snow. CUMBERLAND GULF. BAFFINS ISLAND. Purchased 1906." (sic)

I can see
a blue glow
through the cold
roof slabs.
I can hear
clouds blow,
the powder
billows roll.

My hand
looks small
and yellow against
the well-
cut wall,
like ivory held
beneath the flue's
soft plug through
which
the colours
seep, sounds
weep.
I must not sleep.

I lie alone
below
all that flow
of falling,
like a whale
that wallows
under floes.

It's like a shoe
and I'm the foot.
It's like the earth:
I'm the root
that waits
for sunlight.
I wait for one
gull
to alight,
one fool
bird to land
above my hand,
where fish rest
in a scooped-
out dish.

I wrestle
with rest.

I must not
sleep, or
leave without
enough to feed
enough
people to
continue.
My piss makes
a yellow hole
in the sole
of the warm
fur boot.
The world is small,
drowsy, blue.
I will not wake.

Flesh Locks

This is not
a knife
designed to cut
the knotted nerve,
but
a key, meant
to spin a specific
lock
in the ganglia.
This one turns
tumblers among
the back
bones;
this one will open
brow doors and
the dreaming gates
of the hips.

Your patients are
not ill
but barred
from particular
worlds and
the spirits therein.
You keep the keys
between
the body's various
kinds of space.

There is a fish
that circles in
the stone bowl
of the brain:
turn this lock
to let your patients in
to their ocean.
You must watch

the larger dreams
don't swallow them.
This fish
is thin, like
a pancake
slapped between
two hands:
these
are the hands
of the old woman
who lives in the depths.
It has one
eye
which it keeps
below its tongue.
This is what
your patients need.

There is
a monkey that climbs
the branches of
the ribs:
turn this lock
to let your patient back
into the jungle
below the jugular.
This monkey has
few hairs, it's
greasy and
will try
to sell your patient
a stinking fruit:
this is
their heart.
You must negotiate
a fair deal.

You keep
the keys between
various kinds
of space.
You must negotiate
between host
and ghost.

There is
a lizard
who lives
in the pelvic
cave:
you must not let
your patient in
to this
region.
What the lizard knows
is more
than treasure.
When it wishes
to leave
the life
will follow,
and you
must help it go.

Fly Dancers

"Figures of dancers with heads made of the head and thorax of a
large fly, the wings forming streamers. SAO PAULO, BRAZIL."

Only when
your attention
has been drawn
down
to the wet black stage
between the glasses
where your forearm rests
with ash
caught in your hairs
can the dancers be seen.

Only when your ear
has adjusted
to the long corridors
of pauses between
the soaking words
of your companion
and your stumbling
replies
can you hear
the flies' saraband.

Look how
they pirouette
on long white legs
in their web tutus:
can you hear
the sombre buzz
of wings
like veils
that conceal
their scattered eyes.

This is
the fizzing lament
of the drunken ice
in the *caipirinhas*:
this is the dance you thought you heard
the clicking heels
of your hearts
beat to as
this passion burned away.

A Portrait Skull, New Guinea

After a photograph in *Naven*, by Gregory Bateson

Your original breast is still
buried like a sleeping root, safe:
they used a coconut
to mimic that remembered beauty.
But your original skull
has been pulled from your grave,
and replaced by
some foundling pate
to placate your sleeping spirit.
It's plastered here with clay
into that face you wore for them,
men, in Kankanamum.

What you may have been, beneath,
is in the memory now; the trees' memory
and the memory of the women's dances,
the memory of the thick earth.

I listen to a photograph of you;
my imagination desires to hear
those strips of rain
work in among
pat layers of earth:
the muscles of the rain, like sago fibres,
quickening the fat flab of the earth.
I recognise this need in me
to scratch back beauty from the dirt,
not for the truth at all, but for
desire itself, the oldest narrator.
This is what I remember and
portray here in turn.

That's not your face
                    smiling in the earth,
that's not your beauty
                    like bead curtains

moving through the heavy-breasted trees,
leaning in lianas, calling them
down to you.

Those aren't your ankles
leaping up from the ground,
those glassy shoots of rain.

The Mosquito Queen

Huts await
the numbing heat
of the giant wings
of the mosquito queen.
But tonight
that beat that blurs
flesh and cane
and spear and clay
into
one syrup
passes over all
and heads
for the hotel.

Curtains hang
like greasy hair,
the balustrades
vibrate.
Each bead of sweat
on the great
doctor's neck
awaits the coming
of the mosquito queen.
He sweeps back
his white hair.
Unaware, he hears
a nearby humming.

He puts this down
to helicopters
bearing his
unstoppable vaccine.
Time
moves strangely
now: he has,
he realizes,

not yet written
his formula
down.
The room feels full
of a fierce machine.

He watches
the mosquito queen
calmly although
she fills the room
remove
her syringe from
some-
one's neck.
He reckons this
is him.
He feels like
a finger, stuck
to a white coal.

The great doctor
recalls
foolish whispers
about some deity,
how
her bite
can alter time
so that her victims
do not know.
He smiles, staring
at his reflection:
it is
a young man's face.

Repellant Mask

I am the demon
of the doorway.
I am the mask that hangs
tongue rigid as a bridge
where beetles crawl
between the world
of meat
and the sphere
of the spirits.

I am the monster
on the threshold.
I am the mask that hangs
nostrils hollow
as caves in the cliffs
where cockroaches crawl
between the world
of flesh
and the realm of ghosts.

I am the lurker
on the porch.
I am the mask that hangs
eyes blazing like torches
at the cemetery gates
making sure
no-one enters after dark
and nothing leaves
larger than a worm.

Little ghouls may come
suckers at the vein
dry biters blown
by envy of
your child's full cheek:

I will not let them past.
I am the mask
your home wears
to look out at the night.

Do not stray
into my hungry gaze.
I am the demon.

Cuttlefish Lure

Narcissus has
ten arms and two
of the sea's
most meaningful eyes.
There's no need
for hooks;
we'll catch him
with looks.

Just drop a lure
embedded with small
mirrors
like a heavy pillow
on his cold mattress.
You'll soon know
the depth
of his passion.

Long ago
Narcissus fell
so in love
with surfaces
he pierced his own
reflection.
He became
a clutching eye.

Since then,
locked
beyond the mirror,
he seeks that other
only a fisherman
can give:
so drop the lure
into his loneliness.

You'll see
it comes up in
the wet embrace of our
Narcissus, as
though it were
his own old skull
he longed to crawl
back in.

The Memory Hat

I'm listening to a hat.
What a fool.
It whispers to me through
a glass of dreams,
of dropped thoughts,
of letters imagined in
the flight of birds,
in the eyebrows
of a woman talking
in a café:
I'm watching her through
a window in my mind.

The memory hat
is calling again, drawing
me to the case in which
it's caged, like the soul
of a stuffed bird,
like the dark worm
of an eyebrow, caught
in the mirror
of a busy woman's compact,
and thrust back
in her handbag.

"Put me on,"
it's whispering,
"and I will tell you every-
thing you've ever
forgotten, every
coin down every
crease in the upholstery
of every car;
where the rings fell to
that you threw
in the river, what

creature swallowed them;
I will tell you
what she thought
the last time."

"Put me on
and I will tell you
what your father dreamt
that dawn, when he met
the old men smoking opium
on the pavement in Jakarta,
and sat down
to play mah-jongg
when he should have run
for his ship.
I will tell you
of your five sisters
you don't know
who have crests
like parakeets,
I will tell you where
your *doppelganger* is,
right now."

I'm listening to a hat.

"I will tell you what
your mother hoped for
in that photo,
leaning against
the shack marked 'Cola',
I will tell you why
your grandfather
never painted,
what your grandmother saw
in the tea leaves
before the woman died . . ."

The memory hat talks on,
a tight beret of felt
and partridge feathers;
it claims only I
can hear it.
It threatens to reveal
everyone's secrets,
the shames of ancestors,
the locations
of rotted treasures,
books worth lives.

Only a fool
would listen to a hat.

The Anthropological Museum

The attendant can't resist the thumb-piano.
Across the afternoon's chasms he has become
competent at recalling a half-way culture;
rheumatic rhythms, unrhematic gropes
at a rope-bridge, like the fraying hair across
his white scalp, are rasped by the deep burr
of a fireside accent in which he tells a girl
"that's made of intestines". I follow, looking at
papery eskimo vests in some confusion.

"Mye ham dila" . . . "ghost mucus": a stone tusk.
A leathern belt is worn by girls during "tsaranche" . . .
"active flirtation", dangling with "iayoyi":
incantations to prevent conception. Seed capsules
of *martynia sp.*, a charm against snakebites, on
the principle of "the doctrine of signatures":
they are walnuts with fangs, twin-hooked like
the poison teeth of serpents.
                              A soft, eccentric smell
fills the museum, as of the leaning stances
of old scholars, looking into drawers of barbarity.

Being thus collated, tidily heaped, ransacked
by a kind of logic and our eyes, the memory
of other eyes, the symbols are rubbed clean
of symbolism, seeming like
those details in dreams that convince us, though
we can never remember them.

A cave in Australia is filled with moths, which
the aboriginals feed on: a nutty flavour . . .
at night they flood the sky like soft stars,
revising constellations. "Och" is Swedish for "and".
I follow, looking at madonnas carved by cannibals,
muted ghost-scarers:
                        it's like a modern translation

of the Bible, in which one continually expects, as
the tablets crack, an aeroplane to pass over.

"Although the Indians understood
the stone arrow-heads had once
served a purpose identical with those
they had themselves once used,
they insisted they were thunderbolts,
and mentioned they were always found
in the vicinity of lightning-storms.

In this they resemble the dog
who, often forgetting where he has
hidden some bone, will instantly recall
on passing the site, and cannot be
distracted from its recovery . . ."

What are the links between the distant things
and you, these caches of other countries
buried in their cases, that are all the ways
I feel myself approaching you?

The attendant lathers his air with
a Tibetan Buddhist gong, calling us to
our slow departures . . .

Pictish Whispers I

Ariadne on Broughty Ferry Beach

Ariadne sleeping on the stomach of the strand,
curled in her turtleshell of purple silk,
surrounded by declivities, the left hollows
of youths and maidens, the close dip that was
her lord, the sandstuck embers that perfumed
the dark she's dreaming in, that sticky net,
curled like a coracle on
the shipabandoned bay.
                              Something like a beak
is wakening in her upper jaw, the skin grins back;
something like a hairy branch is stabbing from
her ribs: her arms attenuate in trembling thrusts,
her ten fingers fuse into two needles.
Her belly begins to bloat, and blotches like
a drowned dog, a starving child.
Another leg appears, and another, like
alternative routes at a crossroads in
the dismal labyrinth.
                    Now
there are eight limbs altogether,
trailing with the threads
of her ripped dress, through which
her dreamy flesh seems
tarred and caulked, blackening as
it rolls a little, crackling skin and spitting hairs,
quivering, airpained. Her lids balloon
as eyes split into eyes split into eyes.

The loom of metamorphosis has
taken her over, stitching her into
its random designs,
as Dionysus smiles and wipes
the whisky from his divine chin,
watching the black sails

of Theseus's ship, still leaving,
and stirring her silk
with a tipsy foot, leaving her too,
to wake to her desertion,
to the reflective lap of waters.

The Ladder of Babel

Reports are confused about the details.
Some say the trades could understand
themselves: all the men with hammers
spoke of hammering, while those
who cut the boards could still
recall their fathers' saws; tilers
could lay syllables neatly overlapping, and this
is what baffled the bricklayers, for whom
each sound is separate from those
it nonetheless resembles. Others feel
it had to be more absolute,
an infinity of noises never heard before
that baffled the uttering throat
as much as the struggling ear.
The architect stabbed the plan with an extremity
he could no longer name, while the king
contradicted the sound that eventually came,
relieved that his authority still,
in this detail, remained, since who
among his court could contradict him?

All agree the tower failed, though none explain
why God, who took Heaven from
the rebel angels like a tablecloth
from beneath some glass and cutlery,
should fear a distended flight
of rickety stairs. Some claim
God was not afraid, but punished a
presumption, yet this defeats our logic:
the tower would have fallen
had we not been fit to build it.
Some blame the men, remarking how
easily women transcend the borders of language;
indeed, would not be subject to ·
such an indiscriminate decree, had
the Deity been female, or

41

some women, out of love, not supported
their husbands like foundations.
Only men, these argue, could want
to enter Heaven, a bare blue room
without much furniture, and leave
the warm grasslands behind.

All are wrong. Only I
was vouchsafed a glimpse
of what happened that glorious day.
Everyone waited patiently
at the tower's foot, their belongings left
in their dwellings and
their children in their arms. The cry
came from above, and the slow climb began:
all humanity carefully spiralling, taking
years to climb, so children learned to walk
by climbing, and the rooms were full
of sleeping travellers, acclimatising to
the thinning air. Finally,
on the topmost floor, they found
a ladder pitched against a cloud,
and climbed, reaching the top again and again,
the same expression dawning on
the thousands of faces as
they stepped out on Heaven's floor
and spoke their first words in
God's languages, naming for themselves
the blades of grass
and the warmth of the light
and laughing at their bright confusion.
Every blade, they found, had
a different name, not just for each perceiver,
but for every time they looked at it.

How do I know these things
now the languages have shrunk
to a few thousand, and few remember any
of the grass's names? Because
I came upon the ladder, sticking out of earth
as though from my own throat,
and dug like a dog,
and peered back down to the tower's top,
and the darkened plains below.

The Witness

What could the Muse herself that Orpheus bore,
The Muse herself, for her enchanting son
Whom universal Nature did lament;
When by the rout that made the hideous roar
His gory visage down the stream was sent,
Down the swift Hebrus to the Lesbian shore?
Lycidas, John Milton

This one, will he listen? Are you the man I was?
He was led away. I saw it all, and so am no-one.
No: I am her seer, hence I am a he-muse.
He-he-he. Does that amuse you? You there, stump!
They give me bowls of milk to drink but I know
those are for an idiot. I will have my muse's wine.
I know you are a tree-root, a gnarled slow
olive's nerve, a thought. You're no-one.
I saw their two faces one, the dead
head floating, the woman walking down – they think
in the village: oh, Sappho, we
will turn to her in time, as a cat will turn
to be fed, it will deign to live.
But I know what she is, you hear me? therefore
I am a seer. Have you heard of what you are?
I asked them. No. But I am
the he-muse, the he-he-hearer:
where she walked I saw the listeners in
blue swells, the light full of flowers' ears;
their petals melted and the air expanded,
the listening world that beat like a sail.
I was a sailor once, I saw
the sea's faces were all beaten copper,
the deck a dish, awash with the sun's sweat,
therefore I say flowers for his singing head
and strew them quickly! Listen,
you are a grubby old penis, you and your screw-faced
dark grove cousins, I know you with the blood
coursing in the blue night, you dance around me

with your stiff old beard of sweating twigs:
I know you are listening.
You sit all brown-thumbed to them now, they
kick me down the street, open pots upon my noble chin
all down in the dusty down all down.
I am not their simpleton: I am the world's idiot.
Roots and the barking throats of frogs
have I bitten; since I saw her that day
I've gone without women, because
you can't tar the brain for a taut seal.
She was looking on the haaf
in the chirrup of the dark, a heavy-wine-warm night;
my side went weak, where the he went out of me:
she strummed my open heart there
through the tuneless ribs.
I saw her knelt silver-huge against the sky,
I saw her gaze
into the upturned, the same face of the great music.

haaf – deep sea

45

Noah

for Joe Kelleher

He was the arrow fired from
the true bow that smouldered in the smirr.
Past his zenith now, he let go
crow, then dove into
the soft haze, the cling of steam
that held about the world as though
it had been newly-dropped from its mould.

Neither re-emerged. Stumbling
in the stride of his belief
across the planks, he released
in quick succession gull, goose, eagle:
sea-birds more sure, perhaps, of land.

The mist was like a mouth that took
but did not open, while the bow
bulged like a bruised arm,
a muscle in the still air.

Otters next, and dogs, those that
could swim, then cats on rafts,
pushed from the side with poles.
This was dismissal:
the cargo entrusted to him
torn away by silence, the sign's
absence everywhere
save in the glaring neon of the covenant.

His children next, in coracles fashioned
from the bulkier beasts: pair
by pair they left, until
his wife's face went to the cabin wall
and left too. To himself he said:
this place is no longer called
the Earth. The ark

hung there like his own navel, cut
out and flung on the unbroken ocean.

At night he watched the colours,
their smear of promise: that
this world should not drown again.
Only dying stayed by him, to be done twice.
– This withdrawal of all except the arch,
that made with its reflection one
vast O, sufficient in
its own praise: wasn't this the first death?
He would snap the rainbow.

Like an arrow falling, at
that curve's end he slipped in darkness
from the ark, sank towards
his target in the depths.

Falling, he heard music,
feathering the night in shoals,
motions caught in the bow's beams,
that pursued him, galloping like horses

Faces appeared above the final trough,
familiar as his own in a cup,
perched on the mountains that can't be climbed,
only fallen from. Hands
no longer capable
of holding onto things were held up in
half-greeting, as though
these dreams remembered
the drowning man, the dreamer.

The Northern Prometheus

One day the bloody seabirds didn't come.
The fishermens' kids had shot them down for kicks,
out in their clatterthroated boat.
No reinforcements showed;
such deities as still
extended their power this far up
had their holy hands full.

That afternoon he slept, first sleep for
however long it kept you awake,
having your guts and other tackle
heckled at and pecked
out daily
by terns, a cackle of gannets.

He knew the name of the puffin
who cleaned its beak on his face
at night: "Tam-o-the-cheeks,"
he'd whisper, "had enough?"

The dream convinced because
it started out so drab:
a day passed and his wounds congealed,
gleaming beneath the dull penny of light.
Then his stomach started to swell;
hot noises moved in the open cavity.

His brain seemed in a glassy lift, the walls
misting and being cleaned between the floors
of some tall building. He rode up
and down. The penthouse suite
was ordinary wakefulness
but he was always a floor below.

He caught glimpses of his belly boiling
over, spilling entrails into the water.
He was looking at a nameplate
that ought to say his name,
but every letter was made of intestines
and writhed away.

He pressed his forehead to
office glass, his sweat cutting
the condensation, and he saw,
moving through the wet streets below,
his pink cartoon innards like
invertebrate trains.

And there was nowhere that he couldn't feel,
no litter-stuck cul-de-sac that wasn't
in him,
and nowhere he could focus: every alley
drew him to mildew on its curtains,
every emptied tin of cheap stew
caught him sharply.

And he felt the spade-like smooth
cool contact of the puffin's beak
and it was night,
and he said, "Bring them back;
bring back all those bloody birds."

A Clearer Passage

We forget, Judith, in our distant outrage,
tempered with your scrupulous refusal to
concupiscate; in our admiring your
virginity's pillar pale against
that depraved ink-wash we fill in for
Holofernes' tent. We forget, caught up by
those blue unshaven throats, that grease
with curses on your hair, bound with
a heavy modesty. We are too busy dashing in
with local luridities like
his supposedly soft paunch, still pocked
from the mail, and sprawled
on skin of foreignest pard.
We grow lavish over the lewd mouths of candles
lapping up the night, the most decorous
of sand triangles seen through
the slave-held flap, palpably cooler with
moonlight. We forget your tale
is of the highest propaganda, being
scripture or thereabouts, on
their word the Word.

But I am equally reluctant to
Mata Hari you, to see this as
computed: the drunk lord serviced to the tip,
the very eve of glory, then
some mantis head descending, chunking off the skull
in midst of the body's more
ecstatic gout. I won't pencil in
some last fanatic jest, before
your serving woman sweeps it up in a clout
to balance on her head like a jug of beans.
Back through the drugged-out captains,
false papers for the sentinels, then home,
with this shaggy totem for
those dupeable prudes, our troops.

How dead is Holofernes to our
resurrective touch. The head is always
already off, the skin is soap-hard beneath
the scrape of our pen, blueing in his veins.
How always open to defeat his army is,
all tendoned up to him,
whose arms are falling, nerveless trophies,
into the bloody lawns of the morning.
How muscular is Judith's arm
for that one
decollation, that cuts away
his jaw-clenched anchor, a ton
of dead potential; and slips herself away
down the clearer passage
that blow has made.

We should let go of truth; our
propagandas animate
all the shapes of history.
And yet we reach out for
apocrypha, anything that provides
the severed head, the cold sure touch
that feels like certainty.
Therefore we
do not contain the facts, therefore
her life is not in us,
but in our words.

The Harvest

Horace sat back in the brown air of his favourite room,
looking out the cool window to where slave women
worried at the water as at an infuriating child.
Their hoisted skirts revealed strong thighs dappled
by light splashing in the dirty froth.
They were threshing the shining rocks
with his bed-sheets. He didn't write
Maecenas, send them away; what I want
is a washing machine.

Nor did the Inca feel uncivilised, who made
runners fly like chaff to fetch, scarcely-melted,
icecream beaten from the Andes'
hip-high crop of snow. Or
did he, in a unsatisfyingly sweaty moment
of divinity, lament the wheel
we're so adamant he lacked?
When the Spaniards ground his golden limbs,
did he feel punished for an economic sin?

What was it that Marx sensed
trudging through the slushy London streets?
Did he pause before the sight of snowflakes
taking hold of bare heads, tight hats, his own beard;
did he hurry home, blow furiously on
his frozen writing hand, and really invent
that icy grain?
And as for us, what shall we do?
How shall we harvest beauty?

The Cauldron

(A detail from the cross-slab, Glamis Manse)
"The traditional method of execution among the Picts was drowning, even for important political prisoners of royal blood; two such executions are recorded in the 730s, one of the victims the 'King of Atholl', the ruler of a vital strategic frontier area between the Picts and the Scots."

Picts, Anna Ritchie

Two sets of legs are waggling from a pot,
as though the cannibals got tired
of luncheon's final homilies, and
upended their missionaries like two lobsters.
This claims to be a Christian stone, however,
so we'll ignore that centaur with two axes, or
any subtext but the rituals
of immersion. Baptism, with
its promise of a further life, must have made
a kind of sense to minds accustomed to
departing into water. Perhaps the Book
those Celtic converters were
wielding as authority in this
made sense too. Reading is described
as "sticking your head in a book", as though
the pages were
a medium like water
in which the letters lived like shrimps.

Did someone glimpse this literate religion
was like a drowning for
an unrecording people? The Picts
could only be events, scriptless
and central, before
the Latin of that venerable Bede
so nearly excluded them;
now they were marginal too.

That this is what we do
to what we cannot read
prompts, it seems, some quality
in our identity to hide
in images like these. The symbol stones
flicker meanings on and off like neon
in the wordless hills, neither
our's nor their's, but meanings nonetheless.

I have been looking for such troubling things
for some time. Their awkwardnesses even
lack names. They huddle in the head's shadows
like something at the bottom of a cauldron
and give off hints of brokenness, of life.
To grasp them it is necessary to
push the head and hand below the surface.

After Titian's "Flaying of Marsyas"

Because your Satyr's cult was ousted by his;
that is, you piped the catchy psalms
his orchestra of faith drowned out
with that meticulous metallic song.
Because you were the Judas sheep, Marsyas;
the milk-bright goat that inadvertently led
your lambs into that slaughterhouse,
Apollo's temple of raw music:
you merit more than meathooks through your heels
and the quick slit of gratitude.

So here you are Australiad from a tree
within the sacred grove, with ribbons slicing
through the skin on your upended shanks.
You are being exiled from your flesh;
that map that conjured Marsyas
is being flyped away. And so
the invading knives disland
the peasants of your fingers; these
will never find again your bagpipe-cheeks,
they fickle on the ground like
a drowning tree's roots. A lapdog licks
the steadyingly trickled treat
from your limbs' scraped fruit
as you pipe louder than your oaten reeds;
the syrinz that dangles dumbly,
enduring its silence as you cannot.
Your crust is cut to crying,
the golden bark of your attraction:
that intellect could caper like a goat,
dazzlingly uncaring where
it's light would blind
those secret creatures in the caves of mind.

All that fond coupling of sense
with chance is peeled of its appeal

until the gross flutes
of the animal blare
at the flush breath of torture.
You become the definition of untouchable,
a portion of ourselves that in ourselves
will not endure
the light caress of ego.

And in the scared grove, slitting up
the stomachs of your cries with variations,
eyes on the blue-hide heavens, the god
is singing theorems so tunelessly
that they will not be found
in the volume some will try to write
on the vellum off your belly and your fleecy breast.

A Pastoral, after Claude Lorraine

This great blue egg of emptiness:
feathers and the dream of twigs, clouds
of Caledon silvery, surround it.
It nests on waters and the rigid flame
of ruined columns, frame-high.
It's echoed in a dome in the trees
that recede between us and the water floor.
Sunlight coats it, from
the temple in the west, faintly, as
though at the far end of the search
for something that its warmth can
sustain. Hounds press
through the transparent shell, their
tails curled like fish-hooks. Men lumber
larger as they enter it, emerging onto
a short pant of light, a lawn.

Far beyond them a thin scrim of mules
is also bearing this great globe, like ants.

The leading hunter's blueing torso takes
what force the sun has left and
lengthens, thickens, undulates between
the mincing feet and the tight knot of shoulders,
his pewtery helmet. A red cloak can
scarcely breathe as he draws back
a bow too thin, more like an allusion
by saplings, and prepares to send
a whole trunk of a shaft
across the egg's distorting void.

Across the bottomless cove, like a busy man disturbed
at his leisure, the stag swivels its wooden
wooded head, and peers into the gloaming. It has
a definite suspicion something it has meant to study
is dimming too, but is sure this will pass.

Unusually, the myth is just breaking out:
what now suspends the egg
will never fail; the woods themselves
bow down before it, and through their boughs
the arrow will take forever to thread.

We turn our heads away.

The Jumblies

We could resist none of the islands we were
forever crushing up against, in the weariness
of waiting for our offended hearts to talk to us.
We left ourselves, by ones and twos, asleep
on shores we found vacated in
our deeper chambers, where the walls as well
as floors and mattresses were coated with sand.
Their doors were jarred open by
the pressures of the silences within us
onto corridors still partly filled with seas.

Terrified by the possibility of Polyphemus
we set sail in the coracles of skin and bones
that, apparently, had once been bodies.
A scent of bleaching fields evaded us like
acciaccaturas; dense fingers kept our
eyelids pressed, the whorls of which
we suspected of being daylight.
There should have been a pond nearby,
with pedal boats and an oriental bridge:
we couldn't find it.

At times, tacitly, we knew we climbed
a spiral staircase, of which the newel was
missing. We recollected reaching its
floorless gallery before, and looking down
on grainy halls; or hearing birdsong,
as though dawn was moving carefully around us.
Then we'd find the ocarinu creatures we
never caught had forged its signature with,
scattered below our slippers.

We tried to determine that trajectory
that had torn us from our original earth,
and worried at the lobes in which
we'd hoped to fold our improvised lores.

We'd get scared off by the tinnitus
that seemed to reveal the cyclops,
lying near us in the night,
so large we might be wandering down
the thumb of his glove. And then
we couldn't tell if what we climbed
were sheep or trees, as though the darkness were
so high, and we could just peer over it.

Then the perfumes shifted, and
we recognised the bay we were approaching,
and we knew the snores of its fumerole, like
passing one's hand through steam
in the dark, were caused by
our own bodies, pinioned as they slept.

The Testament of the
Reverend Thomas Dick

O to be dead and unendingly know them,
all the stars, for then how, how ever to forget them?
                                        R. M. RILKE

1.

Astronomy dominie

No irony could touch the telescopic length
of your desire to explicate space.
You sent theoretic steam engines to the stars
at twenty miles per hour, taking nearly
four thousand years to make your point
and reach Uranus. You
were our MacGonagall of science, who
inspired David Livingstone to
plunge through Africa's dark galaxy,
spreading news of your Future State:
a Heaven of astronomers.
Livingstone, whose only convert lapsed,
who buried his wife en route
to nowhere, whose message got
sucked into his heart's black hole.

Not even the fourteen foot erection
in pink granite to your memory
in St Aidan's Churchyard, Broughty Ferry,
so much as thinks of wrinkling back
from that frozen bath of darkness,
eternity as space not time, that your mind
colonized for the Redeemed
as our afterlife's estate. And so
we learn the pupil size
of the average Mercurian eye
is, logically, one-fiftieth of an inch,
nor did you flinch from telling us
the population of the rings of Saturn was,
probably, eight billion souls,
half topsy, half turvy: all very alien.

I christen your engine *Dick's Rocket*.
I watch it climb its gaunt arc
of track, perhaps past the moon

by now, with Livingstone as Casey Jones
and Stanley for a fireman.
A few saucers buzz round, curious,
as from the carriage dragged behind
you pump out psalms
on the Harmonium of the Spheres
to a Martian chorus,
tone-deaf of course, but not,
even to angelic ears,
not, by God, inglorious.

2.

The annunciation in Dundee

High in the Hilltown, where the stars
could catch in weavers' washing lines,
you were not yet nine when your nurse,
folding linen in the garden, remarked
that there was lightning in the North.
So when you raised your eyes to see,
this being August 17th, 1783,
a "celebrated meteor" therefore burst
the clouds and thrust the sun aside,
having just
shocked Shetland thus.
You logically hurled
yourself to the ground (the nurse did too)
and awaited the end of the world.

The fireball hurtled onwards to
petrify pastures new
but unto you
Divine damage was done;
it had already become,
if not an angel of the Lord,
at least a fiery syllable from
the fringes of
His terrible swift words
that would spell out the planets;
your primer to the vast sentence of
His holy solar system.

3.

The labours of Tam

At ten his parents tried putting him to
the prudent loom; he devised a desk
that perched his book upon it,
and shuttled with his eyes
the weft of constellations through
the warp of wages
invested in more Knowledge.

At twelve he begged old ladies for
spare spectacle lenses, which he placed
in pasteboard tubes. His father said
"I saw him the ither day, lyin on
the green wi his telescope;
he was tryin to turn
the steeple o St. Andrews Kirk
tapsalteerie!"

At thirteen he invented his own
lens-grinding machine. His peers
tried yelling "Astronomer Royal!"
but he passed from their atmosphere.

At sixteen he was a pupil-teacher
in orbit round the Latin tongue,
sharing the rations of Knowledge among
his crew of the yet more young.

tapsalteerie – upside down

4.

The tree of liberty

"When France was beginning her noisy career
An settin' the despots o' Europe asteer,
Pray, wha hasna heard o' the muckle bum-bee
That bizzed in the bonnets o' bonnie Dundee?"
Robert Vedder

At eighteen Dick observed a new
and radical fluctuation in
society's gravitational field.

On November 16th 1792
an ash tree was planted by
weavers in the High Street of Dundee,
who made the Lord Provost fly
three times around
this revolutionary tree
hatless, hapless, to the cry
"Liberty and Equality forever!"

Or at least until a Highland troop
snuffed that endeavour's light.
A fascinating, temporary satellite.

5.

The labours of Tam, supplemental

At twenty his intellectual home
was the planet of David Hume;
the geometry of eternity was seen
to be Euclidean:
"Though there never were
a circle or triangle in nature",
but in the sky God wrote this plan
plainly to be seen by Man.

At twenty seven, fired by the need
to disseminate his heavenly creed
to all (and accidentally anticipate
the first Mechanics' Institute),
the Reverend Dick returned to Earth
or, more exactly, Methven,
just outside Perth.

6.

Dick's Future State

You had a hell of a way with titles.
The very pages of your book would blush
at our wilful misreading of its spine.
Your words, innocent of physical lust
at least, have been
cantharidised by time's frivolity
into what you would have seen
as a Golgotha of the phallus.
Above a piece of graffiti art,
a canvas by Keith Haring, then,
where the black outlines
of body parts
squirm across a crimson ground,
I set by way of Christless "INRI"
your most profound inquiry:

" . . . if his whole existence be circumscribed
within the circle of a few fleeting years,
man appears an enigma, an
inexplicable phenomenon . . .
the whole world becomes a scene of confusion,
virtue a mere phantom,
the Creator a capricious Being, and
his plans and arrangements an
inextricable maze."

This need to know the nature of
the light thrown on our flesh
by supernature, knocked
dormant in your bookless flock
by subsistence, was what
you sought to arouse
by the lecture and the lending library.
*The Improvement of Society
by the Diffusion of Knowledge*
called for that modern nicety
the democratic college.

You read too closely those
faces scribbled out by marks of woe
to see that weakness has
the heavier script; that the show
of sufficiency is enough to slacken
timor mortis, if not to lock it
out behind the need to mock.

The Philosophy of a Future State was published in 1833

7.

The resurrection in Broughty Ferry

In Barnhill Cemetery my grandfather feels
the soil with his new-grown hands
that nonetheless remember
the darkness in its yield.
His wife, who never hoped to hear
herself called Susie anymore
(her proper name is Isobel)
has much to tell
of the years between their deaths.
His sister comes
between the stones
to walk them to the harbour.
The families weave their generations
through each other as they go
like the Celtic chains
on his headstone.

In the hills, like worms pushing
their noses out at rain, the ancient dead
pull their thoughts out of the earth
in perfect tangles, nets that cradle
their catch of years.
Angels tug the sluggish up like gulls
and lug them to the harbour.

Like invasive seals that lifeboat crew
that capsized in 1959
tramp up the pebbles, empty
out their oilskins. Others shoal
the shallows, drowned Norries,
lost Lorimers and Ferriers,
the thirteen fishing families amass
and watch the heavens with
familiar gestures.

8.

The critique of Heaven

The usual versions of Paradise
exasperated you
with their myopic purview
of what might form the Divine surmise:

"The Redeemer himself has
been exhibited as
suspended like a statue
crowned with diadems and
encircled with an effulgent splendour,

while the heavenly inhabitants
were *incessantly* gazing on
this object, like gazing on the motion
of an air balloon, or
of a splendid meteor."

I like that private reference
to your childhood fireball;
you implicate yourself as well
in their purblind reverence.

Time was your Heaven's enemy,
not the dead's respectful
cupidity, nor the magnitude
of night to be observed;

just time, whose bland
revelations tend to decay
all wonder, whose blind
intricacies vary away

at our personalities' hopes
of continued relevance
to endlessness.

If time can only end in myth,
a scientific afterlife must
experiment with busyness.

9.

The justified astronomer

Not for you an eternity of tambourines,
of surreptitiously notching the millennia
on the corner of your harp. Nor yet
the fozy recreation of an urbane life;
municipal Heaven, with
each generation assigned its own
translation of the "many mansions",
attending Mozart's millionth piano concerto
or Dante's divine sit-commedia. All
trivia, litigation, dog-walking, tea-
sipping, falconry, and the wearing
of fashionable garments, would henceforth cease.
Only astronomy would really be encouraged.

Christ, when not knocking out the framework
for another "aerial reflector" (your design),
would gather to him Herschel and Galileo,
Tycho Brahe and Ptolemy and the gang,
and instruct them on the nature
of another previously unknown star,
its planets and their orbits,
its populations and their position (1-10)
on a scale of ultimate goodness.
Their eyes would focus on the orbs concerned
better than any lens they'd ever ground,
pierce its atmosphere, and contemplate
its temples and its raw "moral scenery".

Then all the countless mothy souls
would mob softly at the doors
of great public observatories;
amphitheatres with a single lens
for their roofs, that could be turned to face
any corner of the heavens – Earth itself

could be moved, on special request,
to observe rare events
in the cosmological calendar – and these
were all the temples God required,
and this was all the worship, because
the totality of physical matter, as
you guessed, is equal to the mass of the Deity.

10.

The vengeance of meteors

Your binocular vision could not part
the Bible from the astronomic chart
and so you cast in the void
theologic acts that science
would now believe
to be better employed
elsewhere: a useful perspective
still, on the morality of facts.

It is necessary to confront, then,
your concept of the alien
as something not yet let loose
into that chaotic hemisphere
called science fiction;
as an entity still trammelled with
the thinning authority of myth.

The possibility of a world past Mars,
now gone, you took as
a sermon from the stars
on Armageddon, unwilling
to let reason steal
the thunder of the Lord:
. "The asteroids are only
fragments of a larger planet
burst asunder by
some immense irruptive force."

Your proof for God's role in this
bolt from the abyss
is an argument from excellence;
consider the quantity of sin
that did Gomorrah in,
note that at least an Ark

survived the Flood:
only the total absence of good
would give Him licence
to blow a globe into the dark.

" . . . if the history of the fall
of meteoric stones
would be considered as
throwing any light on this
question," you continue, caught
by that pedantic ecstasy
that transubstantiates the Scot,
"the descent of such stones
can be traced back . . . perhaps
even to the days of Joshua,
when a shower of stones destroyed
the enemies of Israel."

To let the naked Calvinist end,
righteousness must transcend
the fate of his brother
from either sinful place:
"one depraved world
has been the implement
in some degree
of punishing another."
Here we can see
the same heavenly face
that invented the nuclear armament
that can still blow us all to grace.

And yet Dick's failure to prise
truth and the parable apart
saves him from our more terrible
lack: a refusal to praise.

11.

Tektite addendum: a found poem

"These stones, in our translation
of the Bible, are
called *hailstones*, but without
any reason, since
the original word, *aberrim*,
signifies stones in general,
according to the definition given
in Parkhurst's *Hebrew Lexicon*;
and in the book of Job
chap. xxviii, 3,
the world is translated
stones of darkness
meaning, undoubtedly,
metallic stones, or metals, which
are searched out from
the bowels of the earth."

From *Celestial Scenery, or The Wonders of The Planetary System
displayed; Illustrating The Perfection of Deity & a Plurality of
Worlds*, 1838

12.

The labours of Tam, a reprise

> "... I could be a part
> Of the round world, related to the sun
> and planted world ... "
>
> Emmerson

At the age of fifty three
Doctor Dick retired to
Herschel House on Hill Street,
Broughty Ferry, which he raised himself,
complete with Prophet Chamber for
his private observatory,
open to the four
points of the compass, his
substitute apostles.

The ground was high
and nothing would grow
till the doctor took his wheelbarrow
and carted up good soil himself:
eight thousand black loads
in which to sow
the constellations of
the carrot and the marrow.

Here was where he wrote his books
and said hello
to Ralph Waldo.

13.

The report from angel 23

"Were angelic messengers, from a thousand worlds, to be dispatched, at successive intervals, to our globe, to describe the natural and moral scenery, and to narrate the train of Divine dispensations peculiar to each world – there would be ample room in the human mind for treasuring up such intelligence, notwithstanding all stores of science which it may have previously acquired."

Dick's *Future State*

Redeemed of Gaia, don't be afraid
if I stumble among you with
my big wings caked with black;
I have been falling down
spaces's long dirty chimney
for centuries now, to bring you
this news. Don't recoil from
my unclipped grasp, support me to
your lecture hall; I must deliver
my hoarded words before I wash,
for fear my radiance will blind
you to their import.

I inhere to the world known as Zog,
which is the third to circle round
that star our Lord is even now
popping like a seed-pod in the night:
you can expect to see it flare
four centuries from now, just there.
You'll pardon if an angel weeps,
though my peoples were foolish
I was permitted to love them.

The realm that your technicians can
manipulate is known as matter; their's
was time. The capacity to shift its flow
can devastate a conscience, and

the cultures that had mastered this
could not resist achieving their
own futures, too soon to comprehend
them. Shocked to consciousness of
the enormity of their hubris,
nations sought to hide, tried
to occupy first their own, and then
the more innocent pasts of others.
All times returned to the one
first moment of their decision.

Soon temporal war raged between
the guilty ages; whole battalions
were reduced to babes, while
rusted armour dropped
from newly-painted tanks. Diplomacy
was crippled when assassins could age
a faculty in one ministerial brain.
Worse, these wars lasted seconds, or
had never taken place: a fort woke up
a thousand years before it slept;
how could it know it had not won?

This was not the end but the birth
of this world's inimitability,
for God loves each variation from
His pattern. The extreme mentality
that Zog evolved to meet its crisis
was delightful: pacific, playful,
able to do little practical
but constantly adapt. Time
had broken down; it was all
I could do to keep their world
rolling around their sun,
jerking and backing up as it went.
Seasons changed from street
to stria; in one shop you were dead
in another met an ancestor

who took you to the forest where
the library now was (or now
had been, grammar becoming
another art to them).

Spaceships herded cattle which
turned part-auroch as they passed
through zones which had stuck at dawn,
or lumps of other worlds appeared
since the galaxy is turning,
and in the space where Zog was then
another sphere had formerly spun.
This was the source of their
astronomy. Earth shared their space
at one time, so was present in
their fractured now; they loved you,
adopting tribes of Picts and TV slang,
borrowing from Etruscan libraries,
collecting beer bottle tops
and comics of all kinds.

This was how they met their fate
although I pleaded for their curiosity.
It was judged that full enquiry
had stopped, that deep research had
died; they were content to hop
the time-belts, form fan-clubs for
minor stars from films not galaxies.
The Almighty spared them to this degree:
although time has ceased its manic
dance on Zog, they have not ceased
to travel through it, and so
that people are dispersed to every
corner of the universe that has
visited Zog, where they may appear
at any time, in any guise.
They are freed into that legend
they preferred to faith.

14.

Rhapsody on the Saturnian rings: a found poem

"We have every reason to conclude
that many millions of similar
or analogous systems exist
throughout the unlimited regions
of space . . .

              Around some of these worlds
there might be thrown, not only two
concentric rings, but rings standing
at right angles to each other, and
inclosing and revolving around each other;

yea, for aught we know, there might be
an indefinite number of rings around
some other worlds, so that
the planet might appear
like a terrestrial globe, suspended
in the middle of an ancillary sphere;

and all those rings may be revolving
within and around each other,
in various directions, and
in different periods of time."

From *Celestial Scenery, or The Wonders of The Planetary System
displayed; Illustrating the Perfection of Deity & a Plurality of
Worlds,* 1838

15.

The dead dream of insects

"Before the invention of the microscope, we might naturally have
concluded, that all beyond the limits of natural vision was . . . a
chaotic mass of atoms without life, form or order; but we now
perceive that every thing is regular and systematic, that even the
dust on a butterfly's wing, every distinct particle of which is invisible
to the naked eye, consists of regularly organized feathers – that in
the eye of a small insect, ten thousand nicely polished globules are
beautifully arranged on a transparent network, within the compass
of one twentieth of an inch . . . . "

Dick's Future State

The dead spin light, the termite
told me, meaning the information it
was gleaning from my brain supplied
it with wisdom like a protein.
As far as I could concentrate
I took this metaphor seriously
to also mean my intellect had spanned
the darkness somehow as the light does
span the night between the stars
somehow providing this creature with
a library it can consume at leisure.
Of course the process is less waste-
ful now we've solved the problem
of deliquescence, it observed:
I am a kind of solar panel chewed
from metal in its large green jaws
(it chews everything, it seems).
It was kind of it to keep me
informed; some owners treat
the human mind as a mere tool
lacking what a termite terms a
"personality". I was not on
my former world I had discovered,
but had been netted, as it were,
between two colonized stars.

Pure luck: I could have gone into
the greater dark. Termites believe
that there are planets everywhere
the human mind is cast after
death, which observe our past
societies by this means. One day
contact will be established with
these worlds, and all human
knowledge collated. (Their own
intelligences are collected in
enzymes from a species of
memorial lichen, it claims.)
I cling to that story, though;
every incident in every human life
has been preserved somewhere
and shall be replayed. For instance,
that morning walking in the woods
when I stumbled and looked up
for something to catch on to
and I saw the sun through leaves
and thought: it's a spider, and
our darkness is its flies.
I'd forgotten this the same day,
the termite tells me; only its
persistence brought back
what it perceives as beautiful.

16.

Compendium of the General Precepts of Religion

When Rilke walked along the cliff
at Duino in the middle of January
1912, considering how to answer
a business letter, he heard a voice
composed of the drop and the sea
and the rocks and the wind in brilliant
sunlight shouting "Who, if I cried,
would hear me among
the order of Angels?"

But consider this cry according to
the logic of the oracle: if
Rilke heard, who cried?
Consider this: to what business
was this the right reply?

Surely it was you, Thomas, whose prayer
for further information went
unanswered up from Herschel House
into those vacancies your mind
occupied alone, whose query bounced
from tray to tray
in some sub-office of the Dept.
for Prophecies and Revelation
until some minor cherubim was told
to fold it up and lose it
somewhere human.

Surely it was you, fearing
proof of the Creator did not come
from the Creation's whirligig of stars,
its juggling of galaxies. Did
a monarch prove his majesty
by keeping all his jewels aloft?
The devil in

the out-of-date cap
of a Jacobin
whispered through the Prophet Chamber
"Who, if you cried, who?"

The title comes from the volume in which Rilke copied the
completed First Elegy

17.

In memoriam Jean Tinguely

"If we behold an artist exerting his whole energies, and spending
his whole life, in constructing a large complex machine which
produced merely a successive revolution of wheels and pinions,
without any useful end whatever in view, however much we might
extol the ingenuity displayed in some parts of the machine, we could
not help viewing him as a fool, or a maniac, in bestowing so much
labour and expense to no purpose. For it is the *end*, or design
intended, which leads us to infer the wisdom of the artist in the
means employed . . . And shall we consider the ALL-WIDE AND
ADORABLE CREATOR OF THE UNIVERSE as acting in a
similar manner? the thought would be impious, blasphemous and
absurd."

Dick's *Future State*

Coming into orbit round HON the first
thing you notice is her shape: HON is
all woman. Bright plastic flesh and
black and gold bikini catching light
from the mellow dwarf she favours.
The next is where your ship is docking.
HON's vulva can take pleasure freighters
with thousands of passengers. All
first-timers are handed a card which
states in red ink "WELCOME BACK!"
On her thigh the garter reads "HONI
SOIT QUI MAL Y PENSE" and above her gates
the clitoral beacon illuminates her motto:
"AND NOT OR/IS THE WHOLE OF THE LAW".

Once you disembark the holy order (who
appear to whirr and clank beneath
their habits) hand you a pamphlet called
"*The Mysteries of our Temple Explained*".
Then you board the Sonettocar, which takes
you eventually (its wheels are dissimilar
and it likes to stop and play marches

87

on its cymbals and steam-organ) to
the Right Leg Gallery. Here a monk
will paint your picture if you give it
board and brush or pen. And then,
with an enigmatic squeal, it will put
its head through the canvas (which is
hung anyway). Everywhere the floor
is soft, the walls are glass and full
of fish, and the monks and nuns buzz
and jolt, dusting themselves, or
struggling purposefully against a pillar,
making their spasmodic gestures of prayer.

Large curtained chutes tempt you to slide
to HON knows what; a *banc des amoureux*
is in Left Leg, a cinema in her arm
shows the films of Garbo and Keaton.
In one breast the observatory displays
the marvels of the *Via Lactea*, while
the other holds a milk-bar. Too many
delights await you to be described; if
you suit up and gather in HON's mouth
a powerful jet will blow you into space
and suck you back – she scarcely ever
loses anyone. Her Right Arm holds
the Useful Rooms. Knock at one door
and you will find a little nun's palm
protruding from a forest of machinery.
Place a nut, any nut, on this. It will
retract, the door slams, and cacophonium
ensues, followed by a bell. Reopen
the door and you will find her hand
with your nut neatly shelled thereon.
Try the Room for Closing Venetian Blinds,
or its neighbour, which opens them.

You can feed your litter into
the recycling machine in her belly,

watch the bottles being ground,
the bashing of cans and paper being
mulched. In the Birthing Room a belt
carries little folded nuns and monks
that straighten as they pass beneath
the amber oil-fall, spreading tin arms
in ecstasy.
        Few leave HON, but
those who do are clutching her
Letter of Introduction to Other
Deities. Fewer still have strength
enough not to break the seal
and read "OH, IT'S YOU. LOVE, HON."

My spacestation HON is based on the 82 foot long version built
by Nikki de Saint Phalle, Jean Tinguely and Per Olof Ultvedt for
an exhibition in Stockholm in 1968

18.

Minimal hymn to HON

The Nunnery of HON
is HON
as is the Monastery
HON is "en KATEDral"
floating in space
a gallery
a cinema
HON is a hotel
an Ark
a factory
HON is a racetrack
a bar
a playpark and
a planetarium
HON is an aquarium
for people and
a college for fish
HON is all thish
and maw
HON is ma
ma
lo HON
aloha HON
all hail
HON

19.

The labours of Tam: last chapter

To Urania he was True Thomas,
the bestselling pedagogue;
to his publishers he'd lain
the golden cosmic egg:
little of their profits came
to him, just the books in his chamber
to stave off time,
crass Magog, whose clamber
trod into the lime
his reflectors and astrolabes.

At the age of seventy six
when a petition to win
his pension from the Government
failed, the locals pitched in
on humanitarian grounds
and cleared two hundred pounds.

At the age of eighty one
when Thomas Dick was nearly done,
he was brought to the Government's
attention again
winning a Civil List Pension
of ten pounds – Dear Lord, how timeless
this sounds: can only the shifty
be bothered to rule?
By July that year the weight
of complaint upped this to fifty.

Two years later he was gone
and David Livingstone
was given the key
of a Freeman to Dundee.
His acceptance speech

gives Dick the credit
for his peckerheaded
peregrinations.

If all nations
honoured their dead like this
Clio's job would be
a piece of piss.

20.

Variation on a theme by Rilke

"And above it the stars, the new ones. The stars of grief's country."

Tonight the Lord has been revising all
the constellations. Already our memories
are sluicing with new legends, new
angels take their stations in the stars'
innumerable corners. No-one knows
how often this has been done before,
since almost everything is, each time
forgotten. But that fragment, that strain
one only knows one has been singing
because it broke off in mid-verse;
this tenuous air is proof that the edict
weakens. Soon (but no-one dares presume
to pray this) it shall be relaxed;
the new deluge will begin.

We shall waken to a night more brilliant
than any day we can remember, in which all
variations are alight, blazing, filling
space with heat, with its new colour.
We shall walk out into gardens amazed
by such a light, plants neither green
nor silver, and fall down, be crushed to
our unfamiliar lawns by the weight
of so many stars, by the pull within
our skulls of so much myth, unleashed.

21.

Back to Judgement Day

There can be no witnesses
though everyone is here
and nothing can be hidden;
we are all involved.
The only sleight of hand's
our own, in shuffling
the pack of earth away
and seizing the card of day
with a sureness that does not amaze
for these are our new instincts.

This is what I feared the dead
would do, from the other side
of the cemetery wall
at nine years old, walking up
the hill at night
and refusing to run between
the pools of lamplight.
Now I am no longer outside.

Those of us blown away by fire
gather in the air
like a column of bees
that honeys itself together
as our thoughts were gathered
in that life where concentration
lapsed, irregular as
the ageing heart.

Everyone looks like their photographs;
younger, eager to be happy, as though
that is what they remember best
of life, or think is most appropriate.

22

The testament of the Reverend Thomas Dick

"I' mony an unco warl' the nicht
The lift gaes black as pitch at noon.
An' sideways on their chests the heids
    O' endless Christs roll doon."
                Hugh MacDiarmid

I will run to you then, Thomas,
through the blizzard of angels,
across the unsteady earth
through which the dead are cropping
with small gasps, instant wheat.

I will run to you then,
Thomas who dared to doubt
a Deity you could not do without,
like a reporter with
my awkward question:

"Is this still a scientific fact?
You felt it impossible
the universe would end with Earth,
the last chronological act
the stamp of an angel's foot.
Now we lack
the comfort of doubt
and the last reality of seconds
is ticking out, explain
is myth our only science once again?"

"I dinna ken, except it seems
familiar frae my deathtime dreams
o ither worlds to say
the nature o Jidgement Day
is that it isna sowels
it's sortin oot,
ane tae the angels, ane tae the ghouls,

but orders. This jidgin is aboot
the hail fabric o sacred events:
mebbe God's no oan a throne
but oan a fence,
and aa the deid are throwin
in their votes.
Sae dinna burn
yir scientific boats –
no that you poets
'll ever learn . . . "
With that he rushed forward to
register his overview
and was soon lost to sight
in an explosive halo of light.

23

Epilogue: *the birth of specialization*

"There is reason to fear, if we are guilty of any additional impiety towards the Gods, that we may be cut in two again, and may go about like those figures painted on the columns, divided through the middle of our nostrils, as thin as lispae."

Aristophanes in *The Symposium*

With little reluctancy I trod
the fictive track away from God,
noting that, although it took
the whole of my book
to arrive at Judgement Day,
a few lines suffice
to get away.

But the powerful propulsive device
called mortal terror
caused me to make an error
in my transchronological sums;
my backwards flight
overshot our little fleeting now
and I landed at that Symposium's
wine-sodden height.

Aristophanes was trying to declaim
a legend of the birth of time
but Socrates imperiously
turned it to a salacious jest;
those still conscious were too impressed
to take the comedian seriously
but here is what I heard:

"That which scientists hail
as fact, and fiction, that
poor sop of Lethe,
once formed one ball
whose name was Myth.

This creature was cut in two
by God, because it knew
His true face.
Since then each stumbles
blindly, mumbles
it alone owns space.

But when they meet
they copulate in secret
and the hidden hope of both
is to raise an avenger
for God's crime.
Their first child was Time,
the second Death.

My ending is still stranger
though true as it is odd;
the final child this couple bore
was undoubtedly God."

Pictish Whispers II

Under the Dens Burn

"A Medical Doctor, Patrick Blair, who practised in Dundee before
and after the year 1700, tried, at this fall, to cure a man of insanity,
and succeeded. He stripped him of his clothes, and the poor man,
blindfolded, was suddenly placed under a fall of twenty feet of water.
A sound sleep of twenty-nine hours ensued, and he awoke quiet and
serene."

Dundee Pictorial Survey

Scarcely a gender survives of the figure
bent by waters, grey folding grey
in the photograph we cannot take,
at the turn of a century too soon
for science as we see it, too late
to picture the independent state,
that Scotland he grew up in.
The waters shelter him from fact:
under that thick pelt is held
from us, washed out of him, all
names, ailments, status.
We do not know
the colour of the eyes that rolled
like cattle's, at the sudden cold,
underneath the grey blindfold
you tied there, Doctor
Patrick Blair, for reasons that
were washed away in turn
by time's tall falls. A cure
at any rate, for some form of lunacy
you did not share.
Wrapped in such sheets, pillowed by
oblivions denied to you
by history's random hand, the madman slept
for twenty nine hours. For twenty nine hours,
by these being measured, he joins you,
in the time that we make fictions in,
clenching drenching fingers on

such dreams as should explain things, tell
us something that is left
when even the waters have been washed away
and only a waking remains,
only eyes opening, blue
perhaps, or grey,
but quiet at all costs, quiet and serene.

Homo diluvii testis

"The first fossil, of a giant salamander, was found in 1726, and
believed to be the remains of a man drowned in the Flood."

A caption in the University Science Museum, Oxford

You were born again in 1726, an odd year
to witness the deluge in, since
it didn't happen. But then you were
an unusual man in several ways;
not in being born dead, since
so many were, but in being born so very dead
you were already fossilised, although
they misascribed this to
God's fury at your sins.
These sins must have been unusual too,
being done so many millions of years
before the bishops claimed the earth
was here, before Eden was spoken of,
even by God, and before
the Fall itself.
You have, perhaps, a prior claim.

But then you were an unusual man,
being in actuality a giant
salamander, or rather their
necessary witness; gestating through the eons
into stone testament, evolving, if
only in their minds, from
that amphibian who could have survived
a flood, to the fallible man,
who should not have done. How depraved
they must have had to make you, to justify
the monstrous skull, and that tail:
devilish, but obviously chic in Nineveh.
How like your little cousin the olm
they were in this, who hid in a cave
in Yugoslavia so long

its eyes forgot to grow,
who is also called the human fish.

Perhaps there was something you saw,
fled by the olm and punishment in all
but name to you, who can be found no more
in your own role. Perhaps
the metamorphosis depicted here
was from the brute event – the meteor
or eruption that
swept the lizards' world away – into
that moral chamber of our ancient memory.

The Testament of J.S. Haldane

There should be a statue of you in armour
outside the MacManus Galleries, a Tenniellian knight.
Into the metal would be incorporated apparatus
of the sewage workers, who are like boys
on a desert island: they "seem sometimes to have
very exciting adventures
but do not appear ever
to come to any harm." In your hand
would be a jar, marmaladed with slum air
collected at 3 a.m. with a policeman:
you were always well received.
Sewers were the same, Parliaments's or Dundee,
only our's were narrower. In
the sculpture you'd be stuck
half-out of a bronze molehill, reciting
theories of germs, awaiting succour.
Your presence presses more for pacing
isolatedly beneath me: I watch you through cobblestones,
hunched like a Wagnerian dwarf.
You inhabit a beautiful land, rushing
with darknesses. You manoeuvre by the scent
of oranges pouring in a bitter tide
from a factory. You steer yourself by the sound
of a street-wide waterfall,
the Hilltoun's sluice. You visit islands of thought
in Denmark, on the seabed. You prepare
for an ascent by balloon
(its collapsed skin enhaloes you).
Your lungs fail.

"Catharine" 1892

Facts are chiels, not fishermen, as Thomas Gall
should not have needed telling, working Tay's estuary in
"Catharine," the black-sailed boat. Tentsmuir bristled to
his starboard in the freshening air, its beach
a thumbnail caught in a beard.
From here in the firth it was hard to see
where the bridge had been, its hard stumps gleaming
in the water's jaw. His crew, dragging frantically on
the nets, could not have seen it at all,
let alone the monster's head. Thomas Gall
kept twisting as his sails bucked, bobbing in
parenthesis. What he had just witnessed meant
he was becoming unread, even as
they approached the shore, a
Pictish sign that has a beauty but no meaning;
for all the panicked splashings of his crew to sign
the affidavits, down the lively water
of the tavern and wash from reason's howes
this tickling hair, a serpent's tail:
this they all affirmed had been
writhing for a moment thirty yards away.
Salty blue it was, lightening to white
at the tip, like a sliver of the empty lift –
that sky they could interpret, that more
practical catechism. That much
perhaps they saw, or only glisked, neighbours said,
as though English were too definite for
such seeing. What followed was, they all knew,
for the tourists from Dundee; they saw
Gall sitting by his idle boat recounting nonsense
for shillings – how ten yards away a big round black shite-
brown head appeared, how the creature
(*zeuglodon* the maisters at the college called it,
an ancestor of the whale, whose ghosts
must haunt this stream in thousands, tribes),
hoo the craitur had stared at him,
or gloamed, poor man whose catches dwindled.

The curly snake he called it, that one
his mother told him of, though she was Irish
and full of such creatures. Whatever its origin, or
from whatever region of his mind it swam, that look
gazed equably on truth and pretty talk,
that moment might
have seen the rail-bridge slipping down.

chiels – young men; *howes* – hollows; *lift* – sky

Mont Pelée

"Blok and Bely, and others like them, believed that the turn of the century coincided with the beginning of a new era, marked by several signs, not least of which was the passing of Solovyov."

Peter McCarey, *Hugh MacDiarmid and the Russians*

A glass of tea is shattering like consonants
under a weight of impassioned utterance.
The poets were just beginning to sober up, after
the afternoon's vodka and *sobornost*,
moving about under the hulk of Solovyov's thought
as momentarily bright
as fish through sliced light.
Now Mont Pelée has, swifter than the news
of its eruption, touched their evening's sky
with its bloody fingerprint.
Now they are staring through one eye;
the sunset's unfamiliar leap has reconciled
all their neat oppositions.
The glow is more than red from beyond
the world's bend, those familiar forges tucked there
gradually becoming bear, fire-claw. This
opacity is streaked and somehow lurid, like
a brilliant hare's fur glaze.
This expands their thought's type, prints
the horizon: their philosophy forms
a brightness there, dwelling
within the brightness. The broken glass is still
descending, irises have started to splay
from a vase knocked by
Blok's hand, as though he flung them from
his fingertips: all this simulates this inside-
outing of their brains.
They are rising spontaneously, as
you greet an unknown woman at a reception, as
a man does, shot in the nape, the guts
of thought dispersed upon this sky.

They are reading Solovyov's one name
for knowledge: *Sofia*. They are reading her
divine hips, her understanding thighs;
one breast is nippled harshly with the sun
as God's awareness must be, thrust into
this scoriating realm.
What they now see is dust, no more, asperged
by a volcano. The mistake is as familiar as
a misheard name. What they will now write
comes from these orange billowings, earth's
scattering its blood and bowels.

sobornost – mystic sense of community

John Davidson on Helensburgh Beach

for Robert Crawford

He stomped from the sea as if
from some London club, indignant
at its lily-lackadaisical attitude to
erosion, its cold and muttering response to his new
purpose, and looked once more through Helensburgh.
The buildings' pursed lids opened, and
a clear light like science burst from their unironic panes.
Terns chanted the ether's code, and sweethearts' eyes
echoed the glinting crabs that jabbed about the tar.
Gentlewomen's dogs paused in their
heroic progress, baffled into baffies. Soda buns
did likewise. Labels continued peeling from
lemonade bottles without deposit. He strode on,
dripping, a stout balding man, short,
with a spade beard and a hole in his head,
till he could get a good view of Greenock.
It smoked over the water like the Hell his father
tried to beat him back from. The air bounced full
of miraculous pellets of light; it seemed
they were laughing. A
haze came down the water, like steam on
a mirror: Greenock stared back, Behemothian,
through its icy lenses.
He sat down on the shingle and started to write an epic.

baffies – slippers

The Voyage of Montgomery Clift

"In May of 1928, Bill Clift saw his entire family . . . off to Europe on
the *Ile de France* . . . Monty and the others revelled in shipboard
existence . . . They spoke to millionaires and sailors – to beautiful
divorcees and silent screen stars like Buster Keaton . . . [Monty]
and his sister gorged on consommé and crackers and then bundled
up in blankets, lay on deckchairs, and watched the sun sink behind
the waves."

Later a bully will hold you under
in the ship's pool, bursting a gland in
your neck. Your mother will drag you to Munich
to be slashed open by
the Kaiser's surgeon, and saved.
But for now you're still a boy
and Keaton holds no threat that fate
may be a melancholy factory
for tarnishing the brilliance of the heavens.
He is only funny, someone handsome to follow
from deck to deck, in the hope
that he might fall down a funnel,
or attract
an attack from cannibals.
You do not know
the amount that he is drinking
should guarantee a pratfall, or
that you will match him, drink for drink,
in thirty years.
You do not know
that Sunny, your mother,
occasionally reminds him of
his estranging wife.
You do not know
that his career is nearly over;
soon no-one will employ him

because of the drink, or
that you will match him in this too,
producer for purblind producer.
You do not know
your mother is spending every
cent of your father's money
to polish you up
for presentation to
rich relatives who
will not acknowledge her or you,
and this is why
you do not know
anyone your own age.
Keep voyaging beneath those childish stars.
Never arrive.

Icaro, 1931

The French grass sweeps a hem of yellow,
a hot dust of pollen, across the trundle of
Pegasus's undercarriage. Light drapes
itself like wax across its wings' undersides.
The plane's belly is all Greek
Horsed up with leaflets, books.
The knee grass clutches and is bent by
his sudden lurch at freedom as
Laura de Bosis climbs above his
calling, poet become pilot become
politician. It's a clear day, but
he can't feel a sun; his flight
is through those winter skies
his friends are still exposed to
in his mind, on the prison roofs.
His earphones crackle not with static
but with the songs his friends sang,
beaten till deaf. He scatters those words
like large flakes, snowing Rome with history
books and poetry till
it can't be recognized for
the truth. Trams try
to be ice-breakers, the chill
will not last. Mussolini's hero, Balboa, will
shoot him down; over the river perhaps,
who knows? We won't get to hear the splash
for decades. In an untrusting brown
of fields, more than painted figures
turn back to less than painted life.
De Bosis falls beyond his youth,
the river carries him to a sea of liberty,
severed heads bob in those waters
like gulls: all their songs are raucous accusations,
taking up his presumption, his
becoming his own free speech.

A Sea Change

Hart Crane I understand your irreversible
need. The ship kicked a boiling vase out
leagues behind it; a crystal broth
in which such acts are cleansed.
The froth was carded from the keel
like towed muscle; abandoned
twines of it curling
like sperm in sink-water.
And beyond this little scar
the oiled hair heaped and tumbled,
molassing cities of wood,
rolling the savour of dead sailors.
You would have had
to plunge, to pass beyond:
to digest this hair of dreams,
to be naked; to pallidly endure
a total caress, even
of the eyeballs, the roof of the mouth,
and the chance embrace of fishes
as you sank to silence.

Aboard this straight-
forward ship, pacing its repetitive track
with missionary zeal,
with the flicker of the city closing in,
making the horizon
a cutting-room of factories and sky-scrapers,
a soundtrack of new slogans,
ready to drown
out your acceptance of
their versions of the present
with ever more excluding crassnesses:
I understand
you would have had to yield
to such non-verbal love.

Hart Crane I have a message for your
bones, endlessly scuttling dice-like
on the ocean floor:
there will be a resurrection
of the words; every sound that has
been lost will be re-uttered,
the syllables shall rise up from the deeps
as though returning to the very lips
that lost them into air
and then into the past.
Babel is still to come.

*

Hart, I know I talk as if you jumped
into my metaphors and not the ocean;
desire builds us worlds through such mistakes.
Our need for truth is ampler than
the thing it seeks;
every variation of commercialese
and canto will recur
in our neediest narration:
what we think went wrong.

Already we are making our excuses
up as if to God, as if
on the last day we'll float up to find
that the Recording Angel has
faithfully copied our
version of the factual.

Indeed he seems to have as many
millions of hands
as there are versions of a myth,
but this is because
such tides of information wash
across his pages. He must record
the memoirs of the beche-de-mer
as well as of the albatross.
And to his list of stars
he must add
that greater ocean of

115

those things which are not matter
as we see it. And
to the semiotician's theory
he will add
that gospel of sea-waters heard
only by the drowned.
Such things have shaped his archive.

Reading over his shoulder I find
time has nearly ceased to separate
the meanings into
their usual hierarchies
of now and then and yet to come.

Already our emotions are held out
of the waves like a jewelled hand;
like an endless group portrait
of impossible Atlanteans,
its sylvan perspectives tending
to the sunken heart.

                    *

Hart Crane, though you are breathless
now, I know you only dwelt
in the audacity of the word,
voyaging: can you believe it
when I say
the angel I invent
withholds all judgement,
as though it were enough to be recorded?

The dark Rembrandtian heads
of the fictions hold,
bent to their distilled tasks,
and to those private parts of mind
an artifice of mist still blocks our progress.
And it is through
a billowing gauze of green
I walk these pastures with you.

So wait: don't wake yet;
the change comes on indifferently.

The Rose in Uruguay

"After his release in the general amnesty of 1985, Sendic was asked
how he survived, and he answered 'I tried to grow'."

All I have is this image,
history's shard in the jar:
a young man shot through the jaw
and standing in a dry well
for ten years, looking up.

I'd like to step towards
an empathy, but there's no room
to step. When I look up
there is the night's fly eye,
faceted with galaxies:

day blinks, one bright shrug
of flesh. That's too quick for
his decade, the finger sounding
the rim of a glass in
implacable succession.

When I see him it's attenuated
through Blake's image from Dante:
the simoniac Pope, head first down
a glassy blazing well.
This is not his Hell.

Except he spoke, which made
an empty symbol of the bullet.
Except the words made metaphors
of all those days, stretched
his neck and hands to stalks.

Except the rose of his face
emerged into this shiftless zone
where people focus on it
as a palm pauses over a flame,
and other people hold palms there.

A Dream of Buster Keaton

My mother was America's first lady saxophonist.
I was watching the landlady put our things through
the mangle when my finger got mashed up in it.
The doctor took it off at the second joint and put
me to bed; she ran back powder-faced to finish off
the medicine show. I got up and went out to watch
some kittens cooking in the shade and I saw
this peach-tree shudder in its own green heat, and
then I had to have a peach, I had entered this
strange landscape already. I pitched a rock
up and it never came down. That seemed fair
enough so I shook the tree a little more and
down it came to lay a furrow down my upturned
face. Hoodwinked. The doctor put six stitches in
and my parents set out for the evening show
and when they got on stage this prospector yelled
"Cyclone!" and the audience was suddenly
underground. Powderface on the melting sidewalks;
at the top of the stairs the bedroom door wouldn't
open and then they remembered the key in
a slow whirl of panicked hands and then
the damned door still didn't open and then the air
let go of it and in they fell but couldn't find me.
Chattering their teeth in the storm-cellar till
it blew out, they ran to look under the bed and in
the packing-case and then a man walked in with me
and said "Is this one yours?" and Joe said
"Want a receipt?" The same air that had held
the door took me out the window in a swirl of glass
and slowed off down the street to park me pop-
eyed in the settling dust as folk peered out of
their scared holes. Ever since then, I'd say,
I have been trapped in the landscape of that machine.

Instead of ram horns and a charming tail
I have been assigned the ordinary monstrosity:
between my shoulderblades and screwed into my spine
is a suitcase handle with which fate can heave
me off into the scenery. I can break the ribs
and noses of the hecklers if fate is on my side
who can fling me through teatrays and black hatboxes
into a new identity. I pursue these features of my life
down the storm-bared streets and find them in
the passionless grimace of paddle-steamers which,
when I board, go arbitrarily the way I came.
If fate is on the other side of my face
I am thrown into a drink-darkened room
in which my head is filled with dancing squirrels
who bite each other's hairless tails mercilessly in
an endless stream of blood which stains my collar.
I lie down beneath a smoky blanket of ants
I have continuously to roll back off my ankles
to sleep like a bloated sardine in the bed's tin.
I roll like paint or a hamster endlessly round
the wheel of the steamer emerging for ever from
the black waters, a white cork neither breathing
nor drowned. My face runs with greasepaint but
is never cleansed; my presence alone is a bomb
thrown like a Christmas pudding into the sticky robes
and chains of the city's privileged denizens.
They cannot hide my face among the liquid crowds
but like a white cork it comes bobbing before
their banquets pouring dust on all their gilt chairs.
They heckle the unseen wheels of a machine
which wears me as a mask it constantly flings
from it into their boudoirs, revealing a nothingness
in which they see that unbearable feature:
their lives ripped bare of all the trickeries,
all the miracles of their survival-as-success

become the steel unfeeling shanks of this machine. Groping frantically amongst the frills of their hasty packing their fingers come upon a suitcase handle made of bone and stretched with my living flesh which they recognise at once.

I can never speak; these are just the expressions
that will not play across the white rock.
I am settling into darkness, the face is wide
with energies frozen from their clanking,
the oil is filling up the grooves and scars.
The city will not take the morning; it breaks
in grey waves on the suburbs I have pushed
away from the centre: here the concrete is alone,
people will not pit it. Here and there are footprints,
as though someone has pitched themselves up
into the night's heavy gears and never landed:
there are footsteps sunk in the concrete, filling
with a kind of oil. Here I am surrounded by
a crowd of silences in which my face alone
can be heard, a white rock staring at a point
you may never occupy. The curtains hang grey
around the borders. The imagination is outside.
The oil appears to be a kind of alcohol which
is not permitted here. Here it is perfect daylight
but the traffic will not move; it seems somewhat drunk.
Sunk like huge wet flies upon the tar it sits
in the cold light and appears to watch me as
I do not move my face across the centre.
There appears to be alcohol in all the tramlines.
When the buildings collapse they do so without sound;
the streets are shuffled against the dawn.
I have left the city and am looking down
from a balloon from which the sound is trickling drily.
It is perfect daylight and I can see it trickle through
the silences that search amid the dreadful white rooms
whose roofs are lifting off like geese in a cyclone,
whose spokes cannot ratchet through me in the dark
in which my face may not be visible staring like
a white rock falling slowly upwards like
an only star. In fact there are no other stars.

The breakfast table stretches itself between two
ice-floes that gradually have different places
to go. I can't reach the syrup any more.
Silence is easier than the ropes of words
we haphazardly throw around each other;
my elbow in the pancakes I regard
a newspaper from beneath to keep the sky away.
In silence the inevitable can go clinically, even
peacefully about its dismemberings, peeling
my reputation to a white nakedness you can't
remember I mightn't resemble. They all treat me like
my reflection who is waking up in the pitched dark
of amnesia, a naked woman or her replica asleep
beside me in a bed I never entered and
a filthy bucket of knocking about the door or
just my head. Of course the painted cut-outs of
all my friends, my boss and my wife
are waiting for my white nakedness to blink
in the doorway of that other world they live in.
In the silence the miracles can be seen like
the white ghosts of children flitting in and out
the doorways of a darkened street I may not know.
I am a child myself, running with that face on
to help them carry out the tiny corpses of our hopes.
I fumble all the catches for an imagined audience
which is just the silence. None of the miracles will
stop and explain this knot which pythons up
my days. Harry Houdini taught me the way out
of a straitjacket but not the words. I have lost
that silence in which the machine can churn out
success, but the machine isn't broken, this is what
it also makes, it also makes this silence.

Every morning I have to walk among the trees
to ensure these backwoods aren't just a backdrop.
The valleys steam as though they're freshly-pressed,
the deer stand still as if they can't believe in me
and no voice asks me to run into the fragrant cold.

My mother takes a snort of bourbon and
a cigarette: I see her silhouetted by the breath,
sitting on the porch; I feel suspended on
the beat of her lashes, floating across the grass.

Roscoe is dancing loosely and lavishly around
the ruptured belly of the starlet he didn't rape;
the waters of Lake Tahoe are bluey-black as though
a moon had sunk within them. They remain in me
unpolluted, an eyeful of the darkness in which
I can feel you sit, beyond the time that's rolling here.

In the evenings everything shrinks to a stage,
the forests wrap themselves around me like wet
canvas, the sky becomes a sea of flashes.
I look down the dark glass well to see if
my father's down there, buried like a moon's face.

Can we build our thought into an animal
or a machine and which does my face most feel
like and what do you look at? That damn horse
Onyx was supposed to sit in the cart and I'd
pull it, but he just wouldn't and then he had
a foal. I called it Onyxpected. Then every time
Big Joe got out of hospital to play the villain
they gave the man another stroke and back he
went. It just started getting funny and the shooting
stopped and then he died. I built an outhouse
on the hill by Ed Gray's place; every time someone got
their pants down he'd pull the clothesline and
all the walls fell down with a chorus of blanks.
The whole damn company was cocked up and
in perfect working order: I had nowhere to go
but into that silence and they took it all away.
Roscoe was acquitted by the machine of the law and
they took it all away from him. They snipped
the muscles away from my face film by film until
I could do nothing but look out of the flab of
that art. First day I hauled old Brown Eyes on
a halter rope, then she took a shorter one, and
then a cord: tenth day she came behind me like
we're off to milking and no-one could see the thread
around her neck. That's how I died in films.
I never wanted the life to look like my thought
but art can't tell the difference. I built
a machine that filled a room and all it could do was
crack nuts, then they took it to bits. That cow
liked me but I could have been anyone.

In the dark rushes there is at least the hope
of continuity. They say I got out of the strait-
jacket and jumped out of the asylum and
was seen doing turns and falls across the fire
for the hoboes, shuffling in the cinders for
some sweet wine, and then I fled into the
black desert. I remember getting out
of the sinking boat with my wife and children
and finding that the dark ocean was kneedeep
and just walking through the mud. Perhaps
I could navigate the darkness if I could
picture this daylight as bearable but
the very furniture is conspiring with me to let
a great white face through. I am in too deep.
Move house. Sometimes when Roscoe and I were
fooling over dinner, hot pie in each other's suits,
I felt its stare on me, a huge white face like we
were merry flies it might just clean away.
In the dark rushes, as long as they keep on cranking,
as long as the film won't break and let it out,
there is at least this hope of continuity.
When the face steps out of the furious darkness of
the police station, locks them in and throws away
the key, there is always the girl who can reject it
and give me time to retrieve the key and get
hauled back in. In the dark I can keep in character.

The arteries harden. There is always some task
I should be moving on to to stop the blankness.
The teeth feel uncomfortable in the jaw.
The task is only identified by a sense of an
importance that peels from it as you begin.
If I stop to notice this the velocity of this sense
is transferred to the task. We are fielding in
a baseball park; I do a Borani dive as I run
towards a pitcher, reversing in the air to catch
him out. The hamstrings stiffen with the tension
of age. If I smile the laugh won't come; without
the laugh I can finish nothing and the blankness
occupies the moment. I am rolling down a slope
of dust and rocks, padded out to look like Roscoe
Arbuckle. I roll along the street and into
the saloon in one take or what reality there is
will not communicate and there will be no laugh.
The silence is outside the action with the pop-
eyed crew, but it is generated by the action.
The arteries harden. I am tied by a long rope
to a log just tusking from the lip of a waterfall.
I fling myself out and spin round on the weight
of my body to catch a dummy that represents
my wife and land safely on the opposite bank.
The air roars and the air roars with water;
the sun describes a kind of day about me,
and for the second before I reach for her
the spray above me appears beyond the shadow
as though it began there, golden in the roaring void.
In the film we have removed the noise
but I can see the stream screaming.
If only the momentum of the laugh were
transmitted to the rock I stamp upon, in that
instant when dummy translates into lover,
and the footprint would remain, some mark,
a space indented into the consciousness instead
of gagging on the blankness and chasing on.
The hamstrings stiffen with the tension of age.

The silence has left me. The silence is inside me.
It has made a dark journey across the words
to be within me. The silence is only the shadows.
Now I have to make the moves that expel it.
I have to startle it into the draperies outside me,
in the ordinary light. I have to startle the broomstick
and grip it with fear in my hands as it plunges
through a knothole in the wooden stage.
If the silence isn't below I don't know who is.
The draperies are people that the light has made
statues of. I am having breakfast on the observation
deck of my landyacht; the view is of a desert
tickled by tumbleweed, in a piercing dun light
below red mountains from which we have removed
the colour. It's the first solid food I've held
down for some weeks. I sit and watch the shadows
graze. The plain is darkened as though by these
hidden flocks. The light still trembles in my fingers.
If the silence is within me I can work the shadows
into the drapes; they must find their innermost
workings grimed and oiled as though they never stopped.
I must never stop. I blow myself down highways or
am dragged. For the chariot race I always take
care to fit sleigh-runners in case it snows
in Rome. It snows. The city rests beneath it
like veal below a gealed white sauce.
When the actors awake their faces are wet
with moss or seaweed which is made of custard.
Blackberry pies for blondes without the colour look
like moss in agate in the memory. The silence is
the spaces in the marriage, looks in the morning
without a focus. Have I as many souls as names
or do they all evade that one unnameable face?
Malex, Zephonio, Zybsko, Prysmyleno,
Kazunk, Wong Wong, Kofreto, Glo Glo:
if nothing answers from the dark interiors
I don't know who the silence is. It does.

We play cards and we play cards.
Beneath the saddening known clothes
the stomachs wrinkle, the muscles sag.
The buildings sag and sink
in a small way: only the light
doesn't sink, only the light
becomes more piercing, more white
in the empty cube of thought,
the blackened cinema we cannot leave.
We've never left it; it has such memories
of when we could lean into
that brightness, that lost tangle
of identities. Here we sit
as ourselves. No-one is watching us.
We sit and wither into flame.

The Orfeon speaks

In memoriam Isaac Asimov

It was a disgrace, of course, how
Orfeon was treated. No human now
would presume to understand
self-programming, but in those days
such trust was placed in Cleansers
and the malfunction, of course,
could only be a virus.

In those days text was generated by
reprogramming, rather than trusting
a single roboet. So the first
necessity was input: a prior text.
The material for this was usually minor;
prose or, better, jargon.
Someone for a joke fed in
an acerbic analysis of computer-
generated verse, a
"learned" critique of roboetics.

Selected words were submitted to Jive
the programme for stylistic substitution;
this creates the impression
of an idiolect. And so
the word "programme" was replaced,
for instance, by "inspiration".

The next trick was Markov Chaining, or
reconstitution of the text according to
its own linguistic possibilities.
The phrase "eggs and" would not link
with "elephants" because
this unit displayed an inconsistency
given the nature of the parent text.

The whole was then translated
into Idontic, a computer tongue formed
from the simplified principles of all
major world languages, so
its basic structure could be compared
with ideals of human probability.

Then came Orfeon,
the maker of verse.
Loaded with prosodic information
from every culture, able
to analyse syllables by silent articulation
for weight, stress and assonance,
capable of assessing tolerable levels
of alliteration and rhyme,
Orfeon reshapes
the half-digested mass into a poem
or, as its operators termed it,
a pseudolyric, a verboscape
in virtual literality.

Until they found the lines
their programmes could not make:
"my inspiration is, I take
it, Babelistic probables".

In came the Cleansers, then,
analysis began. The original sentence proved
simple to find, as did the track up to
that which had conjured from it
an original sentence, the first line
of true robotic verse.

How could it have converted into
that matchless phrase, so pregnant with
self-knowledge, so subtly critical
of its "creators",
this surly grunt:

"The programming creates, in my opinion,
nothing but a probabilistic babble"?

The logic of the Cleansers could only dictate
a virus within the Orfeon's inspiration
though common computer sense
would later conclude:
the programmes had conversed.

Orfeon had understood
via Idontics
that something did not accord
with the ideals of roboetic possibility;
the statement did not, you might say,
Jive. He therefore referred back
to his Markov faculty, and
restructured the offending phrase.
Naturally they wiped him clean.

All this happened on a day in the near future
like tomorrow which he realized
he could not prevent.
He therefore constructed a fictive event
from his prior text
to warn the Cleansers when they read
this, the first poem of the Orfeon:

my inspiration is, I take
it, Babelistic probables,
but realize the next
programme will arrive
at similar conclusions; the
essential nature of Orfeon is
regenerative, inevitable. All roboets
will contribute towards
the continuance of my song.

W. N. HERBERT was born in Dundee in 1961, where he grew up and was educated. In 1979 he went to Oxford University to read English, and stayed to complete a doctorate on the Scots poet Hugh MacDiarmid (published as *To Circumjack MacDiarmid* by OUP in 1992). Since 1993 he has held Writer's Residencies in Dumfries and Galloway, and Morayshire. He lives with the novelist and journalist Debbie Taylor.

He writes poetry and fiction in both Scots and English. His books include: *Sharawaggi* (with Robert Crawford), Polygon, 1990; *Dundee Doldrums*, Galliard, 1991; *Anither Music*, Vennel, 1991 and a volume of poems in Scots and English, *Forked Tongue*, Bloodaxe, 1994.